LOVIN' LEO

Your LEONARDO DICAPRIO Keepsake Scrapbook

By Stefanie Scott

SCHOLASTIC INC.
New York   Toronto   London   Auckland   Sydney

Photography:

Cover: Armando Gallo/Retna; 3T: Fox Paramount Pictures/Shooting Star; 3B: Bob Villard; 4-7(8): Fox Paramount Pictures/Shooting Star; 8T: Janet Macoska; 8B: Janet Macoska/Retna; 9: Janet Macoska; 10B: Bob Villard; 11T: Darlene Hammond/Archive Photos; 11B: Bob Villard; 12-13(4): Bob Villard; 14: Everett Collection; 15T: Archive Photos; 15B: Everett Collection; 17: Seth Poppel Yearbook Archives; 18: Ann Bogart; 19(2): Everett Collection; 20-21(4): Ann Bogart; 22T: Murray Close/Archive Photos; 22B: Everett Collection; 23: Ron Davis/Shooting Star; 24-25: Jimmy Gaston/FSP/Gamma; 26T: Steve Sands/Outline; 26C: Everett Collection; 26B: Everett Collection; 27T: Everett Collection; 28: Yoram Kahana/Shooting Star; 30: 20th Century Fox/Shooting Star; 31T: Everett Collection; 31B: Ron Davis/Shooting Star; 32T: Merrick Morton; 32B: Everett Collection; 34T: Bob Villard; 34B: Hutchins Photo Agency; 35T & BL: Steve Granitz/Retna; 35BR: A. Berliner/Gamma Liaison; 38 & 39T: South Beach Photo Agency; 39B: Stewart Mark/Camera Press/Retna; 40T: Hutchins Photo Agency; 40B: Steve Granitz/Retna; 41L: Ron Davis/Shooting Star; 41R: Jacqui Brown/London Features; 42: Steve Granitz/Retna; 43: Fox Paramount Pictures/Shooting Star; 44T: MGM/UA/Shooting Star; 44C: Etienne George; 44B: Everett Collection; 45 & 47: Jeff Slocomb/Outline; 48: Popperfoto/Archive Photos; **back cover:** Jimmy Gaston/FSP/Gamma.

ISBN 0-590-04855-4

12 11 10 9 8 7 6 5 4 3 2 1   8 9/9 0 1 2 3/0

DESIGNED BY JOAN FERRIGNO
SMOOCH MARKS PROVIDED BY MARY MOLONEY

Printed in the U.S.A.

First Scholastic printing, May 1998

Titanic. The dictionary defines it as "something of great stature; huge; colossal."

The word certainly defines the 1997 film of the same name. *Titanic*, the movie, which tells the story of the *Titanic*, the doomed ocean liner, is the number one box office champ of all time.

The word also defines the appeal of Leonardo DiCaprio. At this moment in time, the tall, talented native Californian is the number one movie star in the world. His popularity is nothing less than titanic.

Who'da thunk it? Well, Leo's father, for one. The story, as Leo remembers it, goes like this:

"There was this one casting call when I was about ten. They brought five kids in just to see their look and if they'd be right for acting. I had this sort of punk haircut. And the lady at the audition looked at me and the other kids. She pointed to each of us, saying, 'Not him. Not him. Not him. You two stay.' I was one of the 'not hims.' On the way home in the car, I cried."

Leo's dad, George DiCaprio, reassured him, *"Someday, Leonardo, it will happen for you. Remember these words."*

Someday is here.

Everything about *Titanic* was . . . well, titanic. The most expensive movie ever made, it has made more money than any other in history. When every last receipt is counted, *Titanic* will end up being the first *billion dollar* film ever released. Its 14 Oscar nominations tied the record for the most ever bestowed upon any film. And *Titanic* certainly made an international star of Leonardo DiCaprio.

His rakish, freewheeling artist, Jack Dawson, was a dreamer who won his steerage-class ticket in a card game. Jack thought he was the luckiest guy in the world. And in one sense, he was. For on the *Titanic*, he met the love of his life, first-class passenger Rose DeWitt Bukater. Against all odds, vagabond Jack wins her heart—or as she put it in the movie, "He saved me in every way a woman could be saved." Of course, the two face death just as their spirits are being born. For all those reasons, *Titanic* was a great love story. Perhaps the greatest of all.

The **Titanic** movie poster became a must-have for fans.

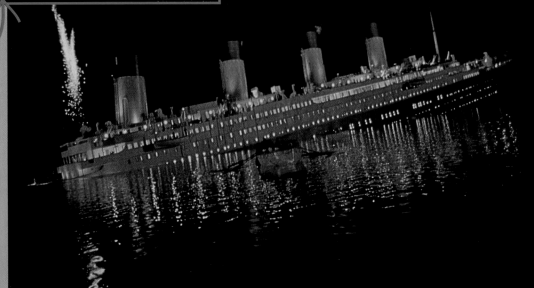

Hard to believe, but true: Leo wasn't sure he wanted to even be in the movie, let alone star as Jack. Writer-director James Cameron explained, "Leo wanted [the character to be] darker, more disturbed. I told him, no, [Jack] is a ray of sunshine. The character lights up the screen and lights up this girl's life." That description still did not convince Leo to come aboard. So Kate Winslet did. The luminous British actress was determined to play Rose, and even more determined that Leo would be her Jack. "I'm going to persuade him to do this," she told a reporter, "because I'm not doing it without him and that's all there is to it. Because he's brilliant. He's a genius."

BEHIND THE SCENES:

Titanic was not a fun shoot. How fun was it not? Check this out:

- Everyone got food poisoning. It was so bad, no one could work for days.
- The actors often filmed their scenes after only four hours of sleep.
- The water—the actors were actually in tanks—was cold!
- "The whole experience made a man out of me," Leo jested.

THE OSCARS®: WAS LEO ROBBED?

Titanic received an astounding 14 Oscar® nominations, including Best Picture and Best Actress. Yet not one was for Leonardo's portrayal of Jack. How whack was that? On the outside, Leo was the total pro. He put on his game face and acted graciously—he didn't comment on the slight. James Cameron did, noting the Academy's historic resentment of "too much stardom too fast."

Titanic is a box office blockbuster the world over. And Leomania has swept the planet. In Japan, fans lined up three nights ahead of time just to catch a glimpse of him arriving at the Tokyo Film Festival. It took 49 bodyguards to protect Leo and director James Cameron from the overenthusiastic throngs of fans ready to mob them. Leo was flattered. "I think the Japanese fans are the best and most loyal in the world."

KATE ON LEO:
"We were the two goofy kids on the set. We just completely clicked. There was lots of tickling."

LEO ON KATE:
"She was my best friend on the set for seven months. We were partners."

BUT DID THEY . . . ?
No. The friendship between Leonardo DiCaprio and Kate Winslet remained just that: a based-on-trust, brother–sister-like friendship. There were no romantic parallels to the movie.

Leo's New York Mets cap was not a prop—at 15 years old, he was a true-blue fan of the New York baseball team. Here's why: "I went to a game and was sitting in the seats above right field. I yelled out to [right fielder] Darryl Strawberry and he looked over and waved at me."

Leonardo Wilhelm DiCaprio was born on November 11, 1974, in Los Angeles, California, to Irmelin and George DiCaprio. He grew up in East LA and Las Feliz—both tough sections of the city. What the family lacked in finances, however, they made up for in unconditional love, support, and encouragement.

Leo explained in *Details* magazine, "My parents never focused on the fact that we were poor. They took me to museums. They showed me art. They read to me. And my mother drove two hours a day to take me to [a school that was superior to the one in the neighborhood]. My father picked me up."

GETTING INTO ACTING

"I always wanted to become an actor," Leo has explained. "It was a need. Everything comes from a need. I was looking for attention and acceptance."

Like all wannabe kid actors, Leo struggled through his share of rejections and disappointments. He also battled against shyness. "My dad taught me not to be shy," Leo reveals. "He'd say, 'Being shy won't get you anywhere.' So I'd imitate people I'd just met who were interesting. I'd do it in front of friends. I liked to act, to become a character."

He started professionally, as many kids in show biz do, acting in public service short films. Leo's earliest jobs include "Mickey's Safety Club" and "How to Deal With a Parent Who Takes Drugs." Then came commercials—"thirty or forty of them" is what he remembers.

Parenthood, a TV series based on the hit 1989 movie, was his first television series. Leo played Gary Buckman, a loner who had trouble adjusting to his parents' separation.

Leo was psyched to be part of the cast. "I always wanted to be in a series," he explained enthusiastically, "to watch yourself on TV every week, to have other people watch you. It's lots of fun."

Alas, there weren't enough other people watching *Parenthood* to make it last beyond one half season. It debuted in September 1990 and was cancelled before the end of the year.

CALIFORNIA PIZZA KITCHEN IN LA'S SAN FERNANDO VALLEY, AUGUST 1990: "In a few years, me and this guy are gonna be huge stars." Okay, that's not what Leo said about his *Parenthood* costar, but had he been prescient, he might have. That's David Arquette on Leo's right: He went on to star in *Scream* and *Scream 2.*

Leo's next foray into sitcom land was not as happy a time. The show was *Growing Pains*, and he was cast as Luke Brower, a homeless teen who moves in with the Seaver family. While *Growing Pains* brought Leo more recognition than anything he'd done previously, the show itself did not appeal to him.

Years later, in a candid interview with *Details* magazine, he admitted, "It was all so contrived. I got to know what I *don't* want to do. I had these lame lines— I couldn't bear it actually. Everyone was bright and chipper. I'd go nuts if I had to do another sitcom."

Leo with Kirk Cameron in a scene from *Growing Pains*— off camera, they did not become friends.

Leo's lovely *Growing Pains'* parting gift: A T-shirt!

He's costarred with some of the most famous names in movie land: Robert De Niro, Meryl Streep, Johnny Depp. But there are others, less well-known, who've acted beside the DiCaprio dude.

Bet you didn't know these actors share a connection to Leonardo:

Dawson's Creek's Michelle Williams [Jen] was in the [short-lived] TV show *Lassie*. So was Leo—for one episode.

David Arquette, with whom Leo costarred in *Parenthood*, also had a major role in TV's [short-lived] *The Outsiders*. Leo guest-starred as a kid who was beat up by a girl.

YOU CAN CALL HIM . . . LEONARDO. OR LEO. NEVER, EVER LEONARD.

THE NAME GAME: LEO'S CHILDHOOD ISSUE

Yes, he was named for the Italian Renaissance painter Leonardo da Vinci. Leo's mom tells why: "When I was pregnant, George and I were in a museum looking at a painting by da Vinci. The baby started kicking. We thought it was a sign."

Yes, he got teased for having such an unusual name. "Leonardo Retardo" is one Leo heard often.

No, he never wanted to change it. "I've always liked my name. It's sort of original. It's the only one I know. Besides, da Vinci was one of the greatest minds ever to be born on this Earth."

No, was his answer when an agent suggested a stage name: "Lenny Williams."

In most of his interviews, Leo would have fans believe that *This Boy's Life* was his first movie. That's because he'd rather forget his first real film deal. But then again, so might you, if you played opposite a "critter" like this one—actually a glorified mop!

About *Critters 3*, Leo laments, "The less said, the better!"

His real-life "critter" was **Rocky the Rottweiler.**

"JUNIOR HIGH SCHOOL WAS MY TOTAL INSECURITY PHASE": Although he is exceptionally gifted, Leonardo had problems at school. He bluntly admits, "I didn't fit in with the people at school. Junior high school was my total insecurity phase." To cover up, he became class clown, cracking jokes instead of the books. "I was frustrated at school. I wasn't happily learning things. I know it's up to you to a degree, but a lot of times school is just so dull and boring. It's hard for a kid to learn in that environment. I could never focus on things I didn't want to learn. For me, it's all about getting a person interested in a subject by linking a lot of happiness to it, a lot of joy doing it."

13

Leo missed his own high school graduation because he was filming *This Boy's Life.*

While working on *Growing Pains,* Leo auditioned for the lead in *This Boy's Life,* the disturbing, gritty, R-rated movie based on the life of writer Tobias Wolff. Leo didn't have a lot of acting experience under his belt—and so far, not a single drama. Yet, after seven auditions, he beat out hundreds of actors for the role. "It was like winning the lottery," he said at the time.

It was more like *this* boy's big break.

The character—of Toby himself—was a tough one, as the film graphically depicts the physical and mental abuse Toby suffered at the hands of his stepfather, Dwight. For Leo, the challenge was not only bearing up under duress, but acting opposite perhaps the greatest living actor of our time, Robert De Niro.

"It was kind of hard not to get frightened [of De Niro's in-your-face screaming scenes]. But I liked it when he scared me. It helped me react."

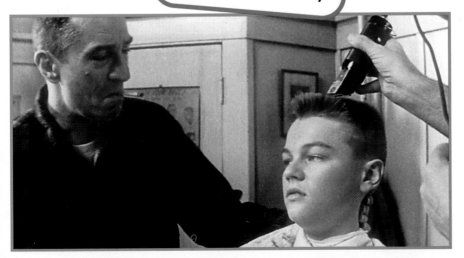

This Boy's Bad Hair Day:

BEHIND THE SCENES: It was one thing to keep up with Robert De Niro— another to surpass him. And in one way at least, Leo sort of did. During the ten weeks of filming, the teen grew four inches, from 5'6" to 5'10". In some scenes, he had to crouch to appear shorter than Mr. De Niro.

15

Want a glimpse of the real Leo in those days? Here's a fact sheet he filled out for *Teen Machine* magazine in 1993. Yes, this is his handwriting, and yes, that's his autograph.

STAGE NAME: Leonardo Di Caprio
FULL NAME: Leonardo Di Caprio
NICKNAME: "Leo" "the noodle"

BASIC STATS:
BIRTHDATE: 11/11/74
BIRTHPLACE: Los Angeles
CURRENT RESIDENCE: Los Angeles
HEIGHT: 5'5"
WEIGHT: 110
EYE COLOR: blue-green
HAIR COLOR: blonde

FAMILY INFO:
PARENTS: Irmelin + George DiCaprio
BROTHERS & SISTERS: none

PETS: Rottweiler dog named "Rocky"
SCHOOL & GRADE: Marshall 11th

FAVES:
COLOR: dark green (color of money)
CAR: Jaguars and any electric car
SINGER/BAND: Lenny Kravitz + Rap artists
ACTOR: Joe Pesci and Nicholsen + DeNiro
ACTRESS: Rhea Pearlman
MOVIE: Spartacus (a real Italian movie)
TV SHOW: Roseanne
CITY: New York
VACATION: My frequent trips to Germany to see my grandparents
FOOD: Pasta pasta pasta
DRINK: Lemonade
FAST FOOD: Burritos
SNACK: fruit
AUTHOR: Winsor McKay
BOOK: "A Raisin in the Sun" ⟵ switch
PLAY: Huckleberry Finn
HISTORICAL FIGURE (Why): John F. Kennedy because of his fight for ending Racism
HISTORICAL ERA (Why): 1960's so many big changes happened
SUBJECT IN SCHOOL: History + English
SPORT: Basketball
SPORT TEAM: Lakers and Dodgers #1
HOBBIES: collecting clothes + sports cards

Leo's yearbook pose. This is from his junior year at Marshall High School.

EXTRAS:

BEST QUALITY: _my humor and outgoingness_

WORST HABIT: _procrastination_

BEST ADVICE YOU RECEIVED: _avoid obviousness_

MOST INFLUENTIAL PERSON: _My Father and Mother_

BEST QUOTE: _From Joe Pesci in GoodFellas 'I amuse you! what am I a ----- clown'_

BEST DATE YOU'VE GONE ON: _To Rosanne Barrs Wedding_

ADVICE TO FANS: _Be your own person & avoid obviousness_

AUTOGRAPH:

Leonardo DiCaprio

MESSAGE TO FANS: clean up your mess!

"*Gilbert Grape* was the most fun I've ever had on a movie," Leo said of the experience.

Gilbert Grape came out in 1993. So did a slew of magazine articles entitled "What's Eating Leo DiCaprio?"
Answer: Magazine articles with that title.

Leo followed up *This Boy's Life* with the quirky character-driven drama *What's Eating Gilbert Grape.* He was Arnie, the mentally challenged, hyperactive younger brother of grocery clerk Gilbert Grape, played by Johnny Depp. Leo's performance, intense and moving, was partly the result of research. "It wasn't until I went to a home for kids who were mentally disabled that I could perfect the character."

Perfect it he did. Leo's reviews were the bomb! *Newsweek* magazine gushed, "[Leonardo DiCaprio's] performance will take your breath away. A lot of actors have taken flashy stabs at playing retarded characters and no one, old or young, has ever done it better. He's exasperatingly, heartbreakingly real."

Leonardo, Johnny Depp, and Juliette Lewis starred in *What's Eating Gilbert Grape.*

LEO ON HIS CHARACTER: "Arnie was simplicity at its best. He was honest. Pure."

Isn't it ironic? He came up empty-handed for *Titanic*, the movie that has made megabucks, but he did get a Best Supporting Actor Oscar® nomination for his portrayal of Arnie. *Gilbert Grape* was not even a hit.

SECRET STUFF: Leo almost lost out on the part—for being too good-looking. He wore a mouthpiece in the movie to make him appear less attractive.

19

HOME SWEET HOME

Leo has always lived in Los Angeles with his mom. He didn't leave home to buy a house of his own until recently. He had his reasons.

Everyone in LA has a backyard pool, right? Leo posed on the diving board.

"A lot of times teenagers are in a rush to move out and assert their independence. But I always *was* independent and free. I didn't have a big reason to move out. I liked having my parents' guidance around me. Besides, it was nice to come home and be taken care of."

This exercise contraption wasn't really used by Leo—except as a photo op.

Irmelin, Leo's mom, and Rocky, his dog: this boy's best friends.

How'd Leo research his role in *This Boy's Life*? He read the book, of course.

Leo played the son of acting great Gene Hackman in *The Quick and the Dead.*

Leo's character was called The Kid. "He was a loud, cocky Billy-the-Kid type who challenges anyone to a fast draw."

On the heels of the challenging but little seen *This Boy's Life* and the accolade-reaping but little seen *What's Eating Gilbert Grape*, Leo was offered a juicy part in the Western *The Quick and the Dead.* It was to be his first big-budget movie. For that reason alone, Leo almost didn't take the part.

He probably shouldn't have.

The Quick and the Dead was aptly titled. It was DOA at the box office and quickly yanked from theaters.

THE BUZZ:
Sharon Stone lobbied for Leo to be in the movie and offered to give up part of her salary to pay his. The actress remains one of Leo's biggest fans.

THE ONE THAT GOT AWAY: It seems as though Leonardo DiCaprio has snagged every role he's ever wanted. Not even. He's lost many for looking lots younger than his years. He didn't get *Interview With the Vampire* for that very reason. The part went to Christian Slater.

THE BASKETBALL DIARIES

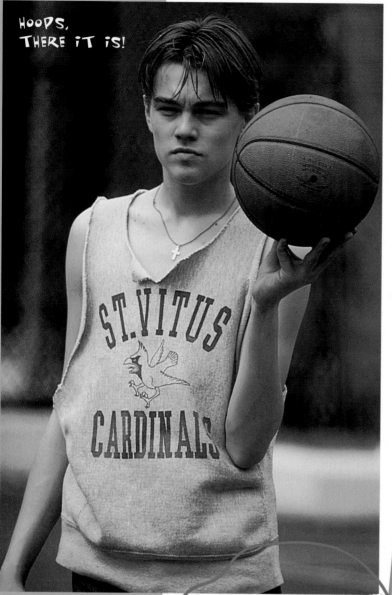

HOODS, THERE IT IS!

ST. VITUS CARDINALS

Add another gritty characterization to Leo's list of quirky, unconventional characters. In *The Basketball Diaries*, he played Jim Carroll, a real-life '70s self-destructive teenage rebel turned poet and musician. "For a person my age"—he was 20—"this is one of the best stories around," Leo explained of his attraction to the movie, which came out with an R rating.

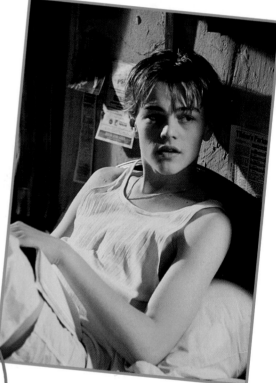

Between Calvin Klein underwear billboards and *Boogie Nights*, the hip-hopper formerly known as Marky Mark costarred with Leo in *Basketball Diaries*. Off camera, the two actually went one-on-one on the basketball court.

Leo's version of the outcome: "I beat him."

Marky's version: "In his dreams."

The modest hit *Marvin's Room* allowed Leo the opportunity to act alongside two of America's finest actresses, Meryl Streep and Diane Keaton. He played Meryl's son, Hank—recently released from a mental institution for burning down his mom's home. A sunnier scene from *Marvin's Room* was set at the beach.

LEO'S LOONY ROLES:
As of 1995, Leo had portrayed big screen characters who were: abused [*This Boy's Life*]; mentally challenged [*Gilbert Grape*]; self-destructive [*Basketball Diaries*]; and just plain nuts [*Marvin's Room*]. What's that about? His fascination with quirky and troubled characters is obvious, but by 1996, he was ready for something a little more mainstream. Good timing: *William Shakespeare's Romeo & Juliet* and *Titanic* were up next.

SCORPIO: OCTOBER 23– NOVEMBER 21

Born on November 11, 1974, Leonardo DiCaprio's sun sign is Scorpio. What does that mean in terms of his personality? Here's a thumbnail sketch of his astro-profile.

SCORPIO'S BEST TRAITS:

- Passionately caring
- Protective
- Honest—to a fault, sometimes!
- Magnetic
- Dynamic
- A great listener

SCORPIO'S WORST TRAITS:

- Suspicious
- Jealous
- Possessive
- Moody
- Quick-tempered

SCORPIO IN LOVE:

- Attracts the loved one like a magnet—the boy can't help it!
- Deeply attached to the loved one
- Faithful when in love
- No PDAs—he'd likely hide his emotions when in public
- Remains true to his feelings

BEST LOVE MATCHES:

Sagittarius, Capricorn, Pisces, Cancer, Virgo, Libra

BUT IS LEO A BELIEVER? YOU COULD SAY SO . . .

"I think Scorpio is the strongest sign," he told Detour magazine. "I think we are very passionate people, with strong opinions—even though sometimes, we're wrong. I don't necessarily believe it's one hundred percent true, of course. Everybody is unique, but it's good to have those little things in life which reinforce some human emotions we may have, make us feel stronger about them. I have heard that Scorpios are unstoppable—so that's a good thing."

CHOOSING CLAIRE:
"I auditioned with most of the actresses who wanted the part," Leo told *People* magazine. "Every other actress did these flowery, mooning things. It turned me off. I wanted someone who would be strong and firm with my Romeo, and Claire gave us that right off."

Never much of a student of the classics, Leonardo agreed to play the lead in *William Shakespeare's Romeo & Juliet* only after being assured of two conditions. He'd have a say in the actress cast as Juliet—he chose Claire Danes—and he wouldn't be playing a retro Romeo, but a cutting edge hero. He wouldn't have been interested in doing a traditional adaptation. "[This is] a much more wild, interesting version," he felt.

It was the version, in the end, that brought many teens who'd never read a Shakespearean play to the Bard for the first time.

CLAIRE ON LEO:

"He's truly brilliant, but I don't think we could be together romantically. We were never buddies."

LEO ON THE LOVE STORY OF ROMEO & JULIET:

"To believe in love and be ready to give up everything for it—especially at that age—to be willing to risk your life for it, is the ultimate tragedy. That's why it's a masterpiece."

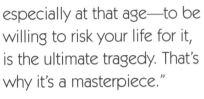

On-screen, Romeo and Juliet shared passion.

Offscreen, the actors got cheeky, especially when Claire tried to remove a lipstick smudge.

Before the iron mask, Leo was the man in the Shakespearean mask.

BEHIND THE SCENES: CARTWHEELS, TWIZZLERS, AND KILLER BEES [OH MY!]

Romeo & Juliet was filmed in Mexico and the entire cast had trouble drinking the water. "We all got bad cases of Montezuma's revenge," Leo revealed. "Everyone got sick." The cast and crew also endured long nights of filming, 90-mile-per-hour sandstorms, and swarms of killer bees, too. It could have been a total eclipse of the spirits, but Leo lightened the mood. He impersonated Michael Jackson, did cartwheels all over the set—and when the mood struck him, hit people over the head with Twizzlers!

ON *TITANIC*:

"I knew it was going to make money—but not like this!"

ON FAME:

"I'm dealing with it as it comes, on a day-to-day basis. I can still go out in public."

ON LOVE SCENES:

"I'm quite used to those scenes by now."

ON GETTING CHASED THROUGH THE LOUVRE MUSEUM:

"When I was in Paris, filming *The Man in the Iron Mask*, I went to visit the Louvre. A group of Italian schoolgirls recognized me and chased me through the museum—so I whizzed by the Mona Lisa at, like, fifty miles an hour. It was kinda crazy."

SHOW HIM THE MONEY!

The *Titanic* went down—Leo's salary since making the film skyrocketed. He's now asking $20 million per film!

A *TITANIC* BLOOPER

Jack Dawson describes ice fishing on Lake Wissota back in his Chippewa Falls, Wisconsin, hometown. Only Lake Wissota wasn't created until five years after the real *Titanic* sank. Oops.

A THREE-HOUR TOUR, A THREE-HOUR TOUR . . .

Just in case you haven't seen it enough times, *Titanic*, the home video of the movie comes out during the holiday season. And starting in 2000, NBC-TV will air it periodically.

LEO LINKS: HEARD IT THROUGH THE GRAPEVINE

Rumors dog Leo like vampires follow Buffy. It's part of the price he pays for stardom. He's been linked with nearly every model and actress under the sun. Most of the time, the rumors are highly exaggerated, yesterday's news—or just plain false. Here's a sampling . . .

RUMOR: Leo's longtime girlfriend is actress Sara Gilbert.
TRUTH: Leo's longtime *friend* is actress Sara Gilbert. The two practically grew up together—their relationship is strictly brother and sister.

RUMOR: Leo dates model Bijou Phillips.
TRUTH: Past tense. But yes, Leo and Bijou—the daughter of Mamas and Papas singer John Phillips—did go out once upon a time.

RUMOR: Leo still lives at home with his mom.
TRUTH: Nope. He moved out two years ago, but he did buy her a house in West Virginia.

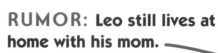

RUMOR: Leo's show biz pals include Johnny Depp, Stephen Dorff, Christina Ricci, and Gaby Hoffmann.
TRUTH: All of the above, plus many more out-of-the-biz buds, about whom he gratefully says, "They treat me like Leo, not like Leonardo, Master Thespian. I need that to maintain my sanity."

RUMOR: Leo fell in love with Claire Danes when they were shooting *William Shakespeare's Romeo & Juliet.*

TRUTH: As if. It didn't happen. Note: At the time, Claire was dating someone else—Matt Damon, of *Good Will Hunting.*

RUMOR: He's a total cutup.

TRUTH: Once a class clown, always a class clown. Leo is the comic relief on all his movie sets. Whether it's moonwalking like Michael Jackson, tossing Twizzlers at his costars, or rolling his eyelids up for gross effect, leave it to Leo to lighten the tension behind the scenes on any movie sets!

RUMOR: He's dating Bridget Hall . . . Alicia Silverstone . . . Juliette Lewis . . . Kristin Zang . . . Liv Tyler . . .

TRUTH: Well, yes. But not all at once [!] and none of the above are current. Look at it this way. Actresses and models are mainly who he meets in his everyday life. It's not unusual that he would have gone out with many of them.

> **ROMEO AND JULIET. ROSE AND JACK.**
> His two biggest movies—love matches with the same initials. And he dies in both. Coincidence or conspiracy? You make the call!

LEO & YOU: THE MATCH GAME

If you met Leonardo DiCaprio, how would you get along? Do you like the same things he does? Here's an easy way to figure it out. On half of each page Leo's list of Likes and Dislikes appears. On the other half, input yours. Compare notes and see how you match up. And remember: Opposites attract, too!

Leo's birthday: November 11, 1974
Leo's zodiac sign: Scorpio
Hair color: Blond
Eyes: Blue-green
Height: 6'
Pets: A bearded dragon lizard
Past pets: Rottweilers Rocky and Baby; a cat named Boopsy

My birthday: _April 13, 19___
My zodiac sign: _Aries_
My hair color: _brown_
My eyes: _brown_
My height: _____
My pets: _Rottweiler Geno_
My past pets: _(Cato) Spike $_
Spaze

LEO'S FAVORITES:

Food: Pasta, pasta, pasta! And veggies
Dessert: Peach cobbler
Least favorite food: Fish, meat
Drink: Low fat milk—with ice
Music: Rap, hip-hop, Rolling Stones, A Tribe Called Quest, Pharcyde, De La Soul, movie soundtracks
Actor: Robert De Niro
TV show: *The Simpsons, South Park*
Colors: Black and dark green
Sport: Basketball
Best school subject: English, especially creative writing
People he's closest to: Mom and Dad
First ambition: To be an oceanographer
First movie he ever saw: *Star Wars.* "I was real young and I went with my pops. It was a re-release. I must have been seven or something. I had a fascination with Chewbacca. He was my favorite character. And I had the little Ewok village."

MY FAVORITES:

Food: _pasta, chinees food_
Dessert: _____
Least favorite food: _____
Drink: _____
Music: _____
_____
_____
Actor: _____
TV show: _____
Colors: _____
Sport: _____
Best school subject: _____
_____
People I'm closest to: _____
First ambition: _____
First movie I ever saw: _____
_____
_____
_____
_____

Leo's message to others: "Enjoy life, be happy, care about the environment and yourself."

Leo's spiritual goal: To learn the meaning of selfless love [you could say *Titanic*'s Jack Dawson knew it!]

In private: Leo writes poetry

A great date for him: Dinner, movies, clubs, the beach, "anything, as long as I'm with the right girl."

Silly thing he did to attract attention: "Acting goofy. Sometimes I'm a complete and utter baboon."

TEN THINGS LEO LOVES:

Going to parties

Being with his friends

Writing poetry

Painting

The zoo

Traveling

Mysteries

Secrets

Winning

Making memories

TEN THINGS LEO HATES:

Interviews

Being analyzed

Being complimented

Making plans

Tabloids

Scandals

Tattoos

Body piercing

Having to trust a stranger

Stereotypes

WORDS THAT DESCRIBE HIS PERSONALITY:

Outgoing

Laid-back

Soft-spoken

Wary

A cutup

Playful

Spirited

Mischievous

My message to others: _____ _____ _____

My spiritual goal: _____ _____ _____

In private: _____

A great date for me: _____ _____ _____

Silly thing I did to attract attention: _____ _____

TEN THINGS I LOVE:

_____ _____
_____ _____
_____ _____
_____ _____
_____ _____

TEN THINGS I HATE:

_____ _____
_____ _____
_____ _____
_____ _____
_____ _____

WORDS THAT DESCRIBE MY PERSONALITY:

_____ _____
_____ _____
_____ _____
_____ _____

LEO IN GLASSES!

He's hailed for his brilliance on the screen, and his penchant for party-going and dating offscreen. But there's a lot about Leonardo that doesn't get written up. Here's what fans should know.

New Year's Eve, 1998, in South Beach, Florida.

Leo got to introduce his mom to Britain's Prince Charles.

LEO ON LOVE: "Anyone I can get along with, I'll go out with. Anyone who has a certain something."

"Honesty is the best policy. Girls approach me all the time, pretending they don't know who I am, when it's obvious they do."

"I've loved and lost . . . but my love life is something I don't talk about."

ECO LEO

A little-known side of Leonardo is his dedication to preserving the environment. He expounded in an interview, "We should all recycle, minimize waste, not use aerosol cans, and try to use less water."

When he lived at home with his mom, he even had a compost heap in the backyard into which he tossed "eggshells, peels, stuff like that," and then used it as fertilizer for the garden.

While he's not political enough to be an animal rights activist, Leo does empathize with all creatures large and small. He has a special interest in whales. "We're killing their habitat and they might be just as intelligent as humans. We need to be more respectful."

At a Rolling Stones concert, he tried to keep dry!

Leo's show biz peer group, circa 1992: Tobey Maguire [*The Ice Storm*]; Soleil Moon Frye [*Punky Brewster*] and Alexander Polinsky.

Leo doesn't normally try to hide from the cameras. A big smile often rewards shutterbugs.

THANKS, DAD & MOM

WHAT'S LEO REALLY LIKE? THIS STORY REVEALS THE REAL BOY BEHIND THE ACTOR.

When Leo started to earn some serious money from his acting, he bought his father a car. In a revealing interview, he described how that felt.

"I knew Dad wanted a new car because he's had beat-up station wagons all his life. I planned a big fiftieth birthday party for him with all his friends. I had a ska band there and polka music. He was blowing out candles on the cake in front of his whole family when I pulled up and beeped, and he turned around and it was me with the brand-new car.

"I couldn't picture anything more beautiful. His face just lit up. I don't want to say that the car symbolized my feelings, but I hope it showed that no matter what changes I go through, I'll always be there. I get poignant about all this because I want to be the perfect child. I owe so much to my parents and the way I was brought up, but I have sometimes overlooked it—and it's something I don't want to overlook.

"The things you did with them, whether it was spending Sunday morning with your dad and eating French toast and watching *Popeye*, or decorating the Christmas tree with your mother—these are the memories that help you be happy."

In *Titanic,* the scene where Jack dons his first tuxedo is the one most fans drool over. In real life, Leo rarely dresses up like that. He likes to look cool, but he's not obsessed with it.

"I don't make a gigantic effort to look good. I do have a sense of my own style—but lately, I haven't cared that much."

That wasn't always his attitude. When he first got into show biz, he was Mr. Designer Duds; these days, he's a blue jeans and T-shirt boy.

THE MAN IN THE IRON MASK

Two Leos are better than one? Fans will have the final say on that when the tallies for *The Man in the Iron Mask* are rung up.

In his *Titanic* follow-up, Leo played the dual role of the King of France and a mysterious masked prisoner who gets rescued from the Bastille. An adaptation of an Alexandre Dumas historical novel, the movie was filmed in France in 1997.

"It was an honor for me to be in this movie," Leo said. "I've looked up to [costars] Gerard Depardieu, Gabriel Byrne, John Malkovich, and Jeremy Irons for a long time."

THE GLAMOROUS SIDE OF SHOW BIZ

"Wearing the mask itself made me feel claustrophobic," Leo admitted on TV's *Entertainment Tonight*. "It was horrible. You want to rip your skin off after a while!"

OKAY, THE REALLY GLAMOROUS SIDE

Leo was mobbed at the premiere of *The Man in the Iron Mask*. Young fans lined the streets of New York, waiting for hours until he arrived. And when he did? Leo graciously shook hands and gave out autographs. "He was so kind, it was all worth it," gushed a grateful DiCapri-ite!

Professionally, Leo's earned major recognition.

What's Eating Gilbert Grape.
• An Academy Award nomination for Best Supporting Actor
• A Golden Globe nomination
• The National Board of Review Award for Best Supporting Actor
• LA Film Critics' New Generation Film Award

Romeo & Juliet
• A Golden Bear at the Berlin Film Festival for Best Actor

ONLINE SHRINES

WHAT ARE FANS SAYING ABOUT LEONARDO? CHECK IT OUT ON THE WEB.

DOZENS OF WEB SITES HAVE BEEN CREATED— WITH HUNDREDS OF PHOTOS— DEVOTED JUST TO HIM.

HERE'S A CYBER SAMPLING:

The Leonardo DiCaprio Homepage
http://www.dicaprio.com

Undoubtedly DiCaprio
http://member.aol.com/Goddess10/Leo.html

Total DiCaprio Homepage
http://skylarking.com/leo/

The Leonardo DiCaprio Unofficial Fan Club
http://www.geocities.com/Hollywood/Studio/6454/

Welcome to Mr. DiCaprio Zone
http://www.geocities.com/Hollywood/Theater/1868/

The LEO Files
http://www.geocities.com/Hollywood/Studio/8848/

dicaprioland's Homepage
http://www.geocities.com/Hollywood/Studio/1192/

Leonardo DiCaprio—God of the Screen
http://www.intouch.com.au/belinda/leonardo/

Cool the Flames
http://www.geocities.com/Hollywood/Studio/6622/

Ahh . . . Leo . . .
http://www.geocities.com/Hollywood/Boulevard/9386/

Leo Land!!
http://member.aol.com/SCTiggers/hottie.html

Beautiful Boy
http://members.aol.com/frailstar/index.html

GOSSIP: Leonardo DiCaprio
http://www.jtj.net/jtj/gossip_romeo.html

Luscious Leo
http://members.aol.com/Tnkrbl777/ld.html

TITANIC Now and Then
http://members.tripod.com/~kingguy77/index.html

LEONARDO DICAPRIO FOR PRESIDENT
http://www.geocities.com/Hollywood/Studio/7551/

The Star of the Most Awesome Movie: Titanic
http://www.erols.com/dimeng/leo.html

Leonardo DiCaprio
http://www.vonl.com/users/steve/leo.html

All About Leonardo DiCaprio
http://members.aol.com/GirlCupid7/index.html

The Official Leonardo DiCaprio Homepage
http://www.leonardodicaprio.com

Titanic
http://www.titanicmovie.com/

Another SureSite: Lovin' Leo
http://www.suresite.com/oh/l/lovinleo/

Leonardo Luv
http://members.aol.com/Burmesse/leoluv.html

Devoted to DiCaprio Homepage
http://pages.prodigy.net/jeweliet/index.html

DI-Captivated!!
http://members.tripod.com/~JaimeandMandy/leo.html

Leonardo DiCaprio: My Romeo
http://www.angelfire.com/md/Rae7/leonardo.html

ring around leonardo dicaprio
http://members.tripod.com/~Valerie13/index.html

NEXT!

HERE'S WHAT HE WANTS, WHAT HE REALLY, REALLY WANTS:

"I want a career, to act, and write and direct, and be involved in all aspects of the moviemaking process. I want a long, happy life. And I want to really fall in love eventually. I am the type of person who wants to share a lot. It's about making more memories."

What's next for Leonardo DiCaprio? "A break," is his quip—and after four movies in a row, that's exactly what he's taking. After that?

• He will make many more movies, for lots more money. His next on-screen appearance is a cameo in Woody Allen's upcoming flick, *Celebrity*. Leo's role is a spoiled young Hollywood actor.

• Rumors will abound that Leonardo has agreed to appear on-screen in this movie or that—when in fact, he's often not even read the script. Two examples: *Slay the Dreamer,* a thriller inspired by events surrounding the assassination of Dr. Martin Luther King Jr., and a movie bio of James Dean. Both were touted as Leo starrers; neither has come to fruition.

• He won't—or at least he'll try not to—become stuck-up and jaded. "It's easy, in this business, to let common sense slip away from you. It's important to hang on to your sense of who you are."